PEPPERMINTS
AND
ROSES

Jonathan Jefferson

PEPPERMINTS & ROSES

S.H.E. PUBLISHING, LLC

Peppermints & Roses

Copyright © 2023 by Jonathan Jefferson

For information contact :

info@shepublishingllc.com | www.shepublishingllc.com

ISBN :

978-1-953163-61-5 (paperback)

First Edition : February 2023

10 9 8 7 6 5 4 3 2 1

CONTENTS

PEPPERMINTS
AND
ROSES

onathan Jefferson

PEPPERMINTS & ROSES

1 |
sweet micronesia

SWEET SMELLS OF FLOWERS.

One gazes for hours, but the hour is not ours to own but only borrowed by the time.

A simple place, made special for a time, for moments lost in seasons never told. Worries cease to care as breathings teased the airs, felt gently in the coves of Sweet Micronesia.

Ocean breezes make way for the familiar, all to forsake tolls of deep blue shadows in the mist, where falls of waters rain fresh crowns in currents of carnations.

Trusting the inhale to release what the chest holds in the rhythm of each breath. Still beating the panes of windows un-shut to its reign at nature's tempo, scented moistures free the dew drops of yesterday's stormy unremembered.

Dreams left unread are the wasted seal to enclose restless clouds so lined in memories. Waves of forever to bear witness the cost of time nonexistent.

Always to be, a world of its own, only in Sweet Micronesia.

2 | buffalo chief

Jonathan Jefferson

WISDOM ALLUDES the restless toils of the wicked, for fevered faces enlarged to reveal the evil roots beneath.

LOYAL TO THE FLAW OF LOVE, hidden in the missing smiles of the soldiers' March. To be the backbone that bears the weight in remembrance of fatherless nations. Still to hear the voice of logic buried in the pastures of emotional greenlands, wisdom for the weary, for it is good.

FEARLESSLY to preserve the greater sacrifice in orders, signed with the tears of mother's heart. Whaling tears water the harvest for winter's passing, yet do the green grasses root in the earth undesired.

FERTILE AT A PERIOD, to nurture the fathers of earth's dominion, baring the stars of knowledge to witness the hearts of men. Shaded in these canopies of knowledge, bearing the multitudes of good, does her tree still grow knowing the forbidden. For there must be more in the mortars' refusal, in the presence of earth's kings of the Buffalo.

PEPPERMINTS & ROSES

IN THE SOUL OF CHIEF lay the missing
pages of the warrior's proverbs once
whispered under the moonless starlights.
To be remembered, does the lion's heart
gladly sacrifice in the vibration of
mountainous prayers.

LET IT BE WRITTEN AGAIN, for now
the words have been spoken in this
place, by the willing, ready and able...
bar none.

3 | great words to think about

HOW POWERFUL IS IT? That every breath that we breathe should sing praise in remembrance of him. Harboring the powers from death to life known by creations' heritage.

For the birth of the swords purpose shall be fulfilled, cutting the contentious stills of rooms, nor taken aback.

Words born of the swordsmith's work are re-membered in them who forge in the heat. The thoughts and words that we speak are powerful waves that toss to and fro the pros and cons of life, when not properly written on the hearts of men.

Thoughts written through the suffocating bellows of perturbations, cloud the minds and prays for every disparately gasping, to breathe the true words of creation only for the swordsmith's labor, will thoughts be manifested, for the commandments of words exhaled them to life.

And the fruitful will breathe life as commandments yield souls multiplied in due season. For the power of life and death lay and wait to strike at the belly of Eve's garden where Adams falls.

So plenty is the harvest in this garden of thoughts unmanifested in dreams of reality.

4 |
early run

Jonathan Jefferson

Absorbing the lights past journey for the reunion of strengths'
wisdom loving lessons weaved forever to edify the swimming minds
of generations in waiting.

* * * * *

Spring's breezes wave the awakening of fresh memories in the
needs for warm of breath from a traveler's past hidden path.

* * * * *

The revealed breaks the fast of morning's glorious epiphany through
dreams of the scriptural laws written on
the hearts of blind souls.

5 |
breath of life

A DEEP BREATH OF ANXIETY IS RELEASED from his lungs. Now, understanding the problem to be more than expected. To see the needs of the innocent unfulfilled, fuels each pump of adrenaline flowing within its purpose of passions. To plead the widow's cause without judgment, for those unprotected by the shepherd's watchman. To be created by the grace of new wisdom, old knowledge to save the perishing fates of ignorance. Flames of glory to purify the renewed strength by words spoken into new existences. New vibrations felt again by the airs and sons of old greetings. Forever to travel where the oceans dew ends at earth's beginning, to be molded by the winds of light, hearing the wise breaths of knowledge in every passing wave.

BLOTTED PAGES OF UNTETHERED CONNECTIONS tell a story craved by illusions of cultural reminiscence. For innocence of sharing years is still not seen outside the hearts of God's kingdom dwellers. Through the tears of mountainous weeping, the echoing cries of humanity plead the case of silent yearnings. Whispers of night fill the minds daughters for generations to be carried, never to cease before dawn's intrusion. Daily love for visits of the most present, for the sole holiday of rest unforgotten by few. To smell the visions of past hunger, seeded in the faith of things unseen. Not to be measured by scales of mankind's pleasure, the upholding of teachings to remember at victory's path behind. All to be passed down for honor in remembrance of the present. Light for the strong to gaze upon the days of wise counsel. Uninterrupted thoughts written to a rhythm foreign to native tongues... are heartfelt.

6 |
night of the sky

Jonathan Jefferson

Dark skies speckled with the life of the night.

Projecting the minds of the spiritual needs of the
religiously felt. Blinded Hopes for the increase,
paid in the faiths full of things hoped for.
Generations of purified minds fail to blot the stains of
consciousness of unshared dogma.

Marketed doctrines are founded in reflections of light, all
for the manuscript value of share prophets. Lost eyes still
share visions of starlight moonlights. The authors
fingerprints mold the glass of truth for the
purpose of evolving clarity.

Making faith the strength of all nations, remembering the
olive branches of our fathers for the benefit of
future reflections.

Past memories, and future hopes are written in the ink of
the present thoughts. For the last shall be first and the first
shall repeat new endings.

For the hope of faith written in the DNA new beginnings
must read aloud the minds of legacy muted by the
Victor's trumpet.

Knowing, all legacy is purposed for the benefit of moons
never to fall victim to reality.

7 | mother of the mothers of the earth

Jonathan Jefferson

Technological advancements marred the face of her beauty. Ignoring the radiance of her presence never will the eye survive to absent her light. It comes naturally through nature to nurture them all, well aware of the pains of birth she wales. Her tears so mighty only if an ark should smuggle hope. The overwhelming instinct to pacify the cries of humanity cause the contractual intrusions of labor pains. Choked by pollution and ever blinded by her love for her suns of her sons. Imagining future stars to be admired even through the smogs of ignorance. She gives life as mother's earth mirror the reflection. kissed so deeply by the suns to the resurrection of future moons to bare the night's chill, soon to be filled with the warmth of mourning. Baring the weight of mountains weeping rivers to seas for protection. She proceeds us all.

8 |
y at a funeral

WHY AT A FUNERAL? Do we say the things our loved ones should have heard yesterday?

WHY AT A FUNERAL? Do we express the love and emotion that we were slow to share?

WHY AT A FUNERAL? Do we smell the flowers never sent in apology? Do we sing the emotional praises of loved ones yet unheard?

WHY AT A FUNERAL? Do we finally lend a listening ear to the words of our very own religious leaders?

WHY AT A FUNERAL? Do we finally give the respect that has always been deserved?

Here is your Y at the funeral of your past. An opportunity to learn, change, and improve yourself, and your relationships. At this Y, you can only turn right or be left in the regrets of your old ways. How long before we forgive?

HOW LONG
BEFORE THE NEXT FUNERAL?

9 |
a million years

As I walk,
the feeling earth spins.

In rotation with the
hourglass's pendulums.

Feeling each grain of sand
beneath my feet as I travel.

Old news as far as the
sun can remember.

Recycled memories trace the
hands of the sundial without a tick.

The broken glass sounds the
alarm of my escape.

Freeing me from the
Orwell of my mind.

PEPPERMINTS & ROSES

To see the past as guided in scripture and respect of
ancestral legacies and still I write.

A legacy of the day,
can last over a million years,
then a million years is crafted and conceived on this day.

10 |
over again

Mountainous peaks shift plates
Taconic to the rhythm of the
pendulum's swing.

Valleys drown in passages of time,
preserved for the benefit of
future inheritances.

Recycled is all for the new
remains unseen
under the rays that increase.

Following the eyes of the night sky filled
with confidence yet untethered to the
reflective moonlessness of doubt.

Jonathan Jefferson

Vibrating ebbs and flows come inspired in circles of Orion's organized chaos in an arrangement is tomorrow's evening.

11 |
all for 1

Jonathan Jefferson

Bold flavors, unpaid favors to savored family matters tamed by old recipes. Plated in patience and served with the experience only life can tell. Knowledge of lessons past fill the veins of the awakened souls as his-story is served cold. Many are the hearts of sacrificed for whence they were watered, green grasses yet grow. Sweet are the fruits of the earth, for there they were seeded and tendered to rest over the sons and daughters of life. All for the betterment of the many to be as one and the one seen through the faithfulness of the few. So we pray.

12 |
lying eyes

Jonathan Jefferson

Unaware of the darkness,

only seeing the light.

Endlessly seeking power,

Unaware of its might.

The boldness of opinions

with no heart for the fight.

Bubbles of confidence

with tomorrow's eve out of sight.

Trained minds to maintain common goods but with

eyes 3 we see what is felt and overstand the unsaid.

Observing windows also tell a story absent the

screened plays of monopolies.

Sprinkled with loving hand and faith in hearts,

the bread crumbs of the ancestors are left for the

nourishment and food for the soul.

13 |
95 floating

Jonathan Jefferson

Street lights glimmer off the eyes of the unseen but heard, balancing all but never fully seeing the increase to be fulfilled by the ungrateful.

Possessing coveted norms to the thirst of those baren and blessed to see truth.

Unveiled ears and open-hearted greetings are the cross to be bared by the gifted.

Suffering lights of evidence to joyous nights with pleasure in the pain's proof of fabricated love.

Unwilling to trust for in seasons they learn to endure seasons.

14 |
g's love

THIS GOLDEN HEART must show symptoms by loves of fever with a warmth of a contagious heart, makes it all worth living again. Reunited in the old presence of faces where new places are always revisited.

Many have beheld in the disbelief and amazement of God's gift of himself shared only for a time, seasoned for this generation. Admiring the strength and fortitude displayed to travel, to learn, to improve, to survive the sharp objects crafted without the custom love of cupid's hand.

All are yet amazed to have bare witness, in the soft connections made in the heart's rythm of strangers. Father of all whos breadless nights fuel the rumble of today's old news.

Remembered by the ease of meals once pained by fatherless lessons. A dad to all man, kind to who are touched, with love is the blessing.

And I have yet to bare witness of the heart so hardened that he if only for a second was unable to warm with life's loves lite in the night laughter.

15 |
good morning

Cool mornings recover me. Acknowledging me as suns rise. Religiously stirring my insides for renewed mercies and the refreshment of my moral and spiritual being. Nights' filter has recycled, and the airs revive a new breath of life in me. The arms of the well-rooted, rise at approach. And I saw a good thing. And I was well.

* * * * *

Like rivers of water, she flows. Filling all places vacant. Vacating the rough places for fulfillment. Her tears flow most powerful, even to dissolve the mountainous hearts of men, and yet are sacrificed at her pleasure. Longing to free. Freeing to breathe. Loving to be.

PEPPERMINTS & ROSES

INTERMISSION

MESSAGE FROM

JONATHAN JEFFERSON

"Nothing beats hard work.

It can even any playing field.

Outwork them."

PEPPERMINTS & ROSES

16 |
true story

Feeling dazed for days, navigating the faces mazed in calamity through signs of unknown ignorance. The gaze of the unfamiliar, recognized only by skewed storytelling of bedtime memories. Curious minds wonder the hearts of broken memories, unfamiliar to the common and alluded. Suffering the lack of knowledge, yield returns unbearable. Glares of unfulfilled passions veil the dis- content lost time. Fenced by the guarded and defended to the beat of the war drum's heart. Vibrant accents of innocent cries echo too loud for the seeing eye to hear. Blinded by the dimness of false light, the desperate eyes of the famished graze history pastures in search of untethered purity. Rays of truth uncovered but obscured by arterial perspectives. Love yourself. Seek the truth. Live the life.

17 |refreshing tears

PEPPERMINTS & ROSES

Scampering to take cover as storms rage above.

Causing small problems to magnify in the mind's eye, where rain drops descend yet feel like buckets of reassurssion.

For purity they carry the gift of a new beginning.

Providing for all a personal portion of life life's graceful purpose.

To be recalled by the sun from whence it came.

Unseen and alternatively routed to the eyes of destiny's redundant cry.

As vapors rise the air thickens with anticipation of future storms to come. And it is good.

18 |
medicine cookies

PEPPERMINTS & ROSES

I swallow each one with a smile. Not easy but necessary.

Awfully bitter and they never go down easy,

yet I digest every moment,

cherish every ache and smile through the pain.

No tears, no fear, no idea what's next but one thing I know for

sure... I look forward to it. Bring it on!

Hard times only make me stronger. So I endure.

Now knowing the smell, the taste, and feel of fire affords me a

story to tell only to the willing ear and genuine heart. Tested by

ears, eyes and hearts weighted in solitude.

If I'm crying, what will the women and children do.

No tears. No fears. No problem. I'll just have another one of

those cookies, starting to get use to the taste.

19 |
spilled
tea time

PEPPERMINTS & ROSES

SO GOOD TO ME but yet alludes me.

Wasted and pressed,
preserved for the best of,
zoned and measured,
reserved for pleasure,
gray hairs teach us better but whatever.

Watched, clocked and tethered,
we hope for a better, when in comes stormy weather.

The most high said pray now and forever.

For-time-just-is.

No need to take, for each moment is yours to taste,
waste, pace, and so we pray.

The one in which we live,
and the ones we choose to give,
is when we actually lived.

Counted in seconds,
each considered a blessing but how many miss the lesson.

Time is the blessing.

20 | tears of life

PEPPERMINTS & ROSES

Rainy mornings rejuvenate the mind's eye. Washing away past

memories while refreshing future dreams. And in solitude all is a

new! Synchronized tear drops play alone the window pane as

Redundant as history's lessons unlearned. They play the familiar

song of destiny's futures. Seeded in the souls of mothers, with smiles

from on high, for surety of an abundant increase. As earth shuffles

the Taconic deck to welcome a new sun rise all is multiplied. Moons

watchful evenings, shadow full cycles of passing seasons to come.

Futures' dreams of impossibilities are refreshed.

So We are renewed and so We are.

21 | his hands

FATHER, guide my hand and greet my heart
with your love. Above and below,
before me and beyond
GOD CARRY ME.

Near rivers, through deserts,
on mountains literally.
GOD CARRY ME.

Iraq, South Africa, Germany and Greece
and even more than you see,
before and beyond me,
GOD CARRIED ME.

Believe and see but don't just listen to me.
What I know for sure is that
GOD CARRIED ME.

22 |
remember
the time

Remembering a time when neighbors were family and family were guests.

Remembering a time when brothers and sisters were united without being related, bonds created and somehow, we made it.

Remembering a time when most fights started because someone was 'sticking their chest out' a little too far but ended with life long friendships.

Remembering a time when family bonds were secret and last names held protected honor.

Remembering a time when your word was bond and respect was earned.

Remember, that time is too short to waste so enjoy, encourage and embrace life one second at a time.

23 | good night

PEPPERMINTS & ROSES

Cool nights unwind me. Washing away the

tempered issues of the day. My Canopyed stars fill

the sky more brilliantly than the most spectacular

light show, custom for bedtime memories skyed in

place solely by the most high. Dressed in the

silence of humility. For days past carry not the

lessons of the present, to lived and learned with

love. True, untether to the wondered distractions,

feed to the slaughtered minds of ignorance foretold.

Directed dreams to heal the unfilled masses of

minds that thirst. For the host of serving the humble

in wisdoms' tone.

24 |
letter to a black soldier

PEPPERMINTS & ROSES

Hey Soldier! You had one mission and you are failing. The mission was simple and clear. Protect these women and children!!! No one said it would be easy. No one even said that you would survive the mission, but you are still breathing, right? You were knocked out, unconscience and woke up not knowing who you are, where you are, or what mission you are here to accomplish. Well, I'm here to remind you. Protect these women and children at all costs!

* * * * *

Let me explain how we have been surviving so far. We were attacked by ship, taken prisoner. As POWs, we endured pain, torture, rape, mutilation, slavery, drugs, alcohol, Tuskegee and other experiments, Jim Crow, Redlining, jury mandering, media defamation, industrial prison complexes, false imprisonments, assassinations, theft of both intellectual and physical property including our own bodies. We were deprived of our names, history, heritage, families, and languages. There has been unmeasurable bloodshed and much much more. Women and children were captured along with us and thank God for them! You see, the women kept us from drowning. She tied some pieces of wood together and started kicking to keep us afloat. Even while being pursued and beaten, she just kept kicking. Raped, cursed, she just kept kicking unprotected, and abused...she just kept kicking. She found us floating, knocked out, then she gave us mouth-to-mouth because she knew God's love was the only thing that could save us.

When I woke up, I saw her unprotected, being pursued, beaten, raped, and abused still. Different methods are being used but to the same results. I know you might want a little time to wake up, recover and regain some strength but I need some backup. I saw how out-numbered we were so I went to law school to get some extra ammo.

Just watch my back, just cover my 6! All those scars on my back, those aren't from some slave master's whip. Those are from all the knives I pulled out on the way to you but God told me, where two or three be gathered in his name, he would be in the mist then he led me to you. So rise up and walk! If not... the pleasure is all mine but I gotta keep moving. I gotta protect these women and children!

25 | cappuccino

Jonathan Jefferson

Hello,

My wife and I visited your hotel back in 2018 after we got married and we had the time of our lives. The staff was so friendly that we felt like part of the family.

The cafe downstairs... it blew us away. The cappuccino is still the best I have ever had. It was our first time in South Africa and that cappuccino was just priceless.

Thank you so much! It was an experience that we will never ever forget.

Thank you so much. We appreciate the feedback.

So how is your wife?

Well, my wife is ill now. I do all I can, to keep her comfortable, to keep her smiling.

It is funny... Yesterday, her nurse asked me how I stayed so motivated.

She said that most husbands don't bother to hang around.

PEPPERMINTS & ROSES

Well, what did you say?

I just took a sip from my coffee cup.

She wouldn't understand that the taste of cappuccino still reminds me of South Africa.

26 | farewell

PEPPERMINTS & ROSES

It's that feeling you have when you know you're about to reach the top but you can't help yourself but to reach back trying to pull as many as possible with you. But they slap your hand away. Again and again, they slap it away. Eventually, and you know this, your hand will be too soar to continue your climb to the next level.

There has to be a way!

Maybe we just haven't found their niche yet.
Maybe school or credit repair or maybe one of those life coaches might help... I don't know. Maybe it's your mindset?
Maybe I have to continue alone... but I always imagined us reaching the top together.

Sink or swim!
Ride or die!
Bar none.

Jonathan Jefferson

Well it's obvious to me that this is where we part ways.

Just know the Love that I showed you was real.

Every second,

every joke,

every laugh and

every embrace.

Farewell

27 |
uncle jon-jon

Jonathan Jefferson

Uncle Jon-Jon
Being here and there,
to explain the unfair knowings
in the eyes of men.
This evidence of truth,
sparked by the lighting of places
filled without importance no more.
Awakening the self above
understanding of lessons
missed in translation.
Always to speak
the wanted over miles past,
only to be repeated in the remembrance.
Larger in the eyes of the imagined,
strengths hidden in the tides
of weathered survivals.
For the forgotten words of tears,
forever to cleanse
the shouldered hearts of despair.
In the timeless words of fallen ears,
never to ring the faithful hands
of the sundial.
For the one,
there must be many,
for the many will be as one.

28 | survival speech

Why do people go through life feeling as if they are failing? Allowing others to gage your success in life. Success has a different meaning for everyone but we collectively have allowed others to dictate our dreams of a successful life, marriage, relationship, and career. Which is better? Being unhappy and surrounded by money or doing what you truly love for a living? Doing what you love to do is winning and wealth that truly improves your quality of life.

Winning or losing is consistently dependent on a goal. What is your goal? Have you written a plan? Having the plan in your head may help you focus on your vision but writing it down is like signing the bottom of a check. It solidifies, strengthens, and represents the physical manifestation of your goal or dream. You cannot fail if you just keep trying, you never stop trying as long as you are breathing. This is unconditional. It's called survival.

29 |
veterans only

ROGER THAT! Unequip with the MOS needed to PMCS the mindset of survival after... Feeling as a POW in your own rear D. To guard the nation against those too far, deploy again and return to cheer the anthems.

Toasting the canteens of confusion against the wine glasses of political fabrications. Raised to the painful clash of ears for things seen and not read. Answering the memories, never to qualify breaths borrowed from the angels of the grave. Brave of the honor, colors in mayhem, for the sake of revealing some truths, truths the hard way... traced within the darkest exhale with fevers uncured by humanity's sick call.

O dark 30 to the morning of branded choices on the hearts and minds of the stop loss. From ETAs to PCS for better BAH and BAS, and no

PEPPERMINTS & ROSES

BS from CMS and LTs with PTSD. To NO GO the future plans at their place of birth, No CS2 will blind the focused and needy by history's operational control of self. With screens of smoke, the genius of wealth is DX-ed in the orders of those once led and trained by VETERANS.

30 |
under weight

PEPPERMINTS & ROSES

Rays of renewed mercy feed the unsubmerged horizons of her garden. Deep blues waves concealing all still hidden in a times capsule, revealing each grain of sand in due seasons of un-dated visions.

Whispers from the belly of the befriended to burden the suns of many. Her-story told only through the eye of the afflicted, is not drowned by the echoing cries of morning night's summons.

Now feeding the hungry of generations, a time has come to break the fast of yesterday's imperfections. Yearning for returns reserved for the hands of the righteous works of the heart. Read from her tables, are the weighing on the scales feathered before us.

PEPPERMINTS & ROSES

ABOUT THE AUTHOR

PEPPERMINTS & ROSES

Jonathan Jefferson

J onathan Jefferson was born in Chicago, Illinois, on May 23rd to the parents of Gloria Jefferson-Jones and George Grant.

Jefferson holds an A.A. and B.A., both in Business Administration Management. He values his accomplishments in education, religious studies, and military service. Jefferson's experiences led him to the ultimate fate of becoming an author and poetry writer. His passion for quality of life has undoubtedly contributed to what he will share with the world through the "J.J. Projects," which will include more poetry and the traditional book publication of memoirs of his life. He will inspire and motivate us to take hold of the 24 hours we have each day.

PEPPERMINTS & ROSES

If you know Jefferson, you may say he is intelligent, fun, and even a little silly. Many don't know, but he played the handbells in grade school and enjoyed it. Jefferson is passionate about quality of life, and he is a phenomenal public speaker.

As the CEO of M.R. SECURITY SOLUTIONS, LLC, Jefferson has a philosophy that nothing beats hard work. It can even any playing field. So, outwork them. Family, community, city, state, country, world, and the universe are all small to the creator. We are one.

Jonathan Jefferson

PEPPERMINTS & ROSES

Jonathan Jefferson

Printed in the USA
CPSIA information can be obtained
at www.ICGtesting.com
CBHW040207231024
16172CB00008B/33